~~~~~ ABC ~~~~~
of Crawlers and Flyers

photographs and text by Hope Ryden

Clarion Books/New York

Clarion Books
a Houghton Mifflin Company imprint
215 Park Avenue South, New York, NY 10003
Text and photographs copyright © 1996 by Hope Ryden

Type is set in 14/17-pt. Horley.

Title page photograph: Ladybug.

For information about this and other Houghton Mifflin trade and reference books
and multimedia products, visit The Bookstore at Houghton Mifflin on
the World Wide Web at (http://www.hmco.com/trade/).

Printed in Singapore

Library of Congress Cataloging-in-Publication Data

Ryden, Hope.
ABC of crawlers and flyers / by Hope Ryden.
p. cm.
Summary: Illustrations and text present a different insect for each letter of
the alphabet, from ants and aphids to zebra longwing.
ISBN 0-395-72808-8
1. Insects—Juvenile literature. 2. English language—Alphabet—Juvenile literature.
[1. Insects. 2. Alphabet.] I. Title.
QL467.2.R94 1993
595.7[E]—dc20
95-45676
CIP
AC

TWP 10 9 8 7 6 5 4 3 2 1

For Nathaniel Combs, Jr.,
who found the elusive praying mantis

Introduction

Did you know that millions of tiny beings live in fields, forests, vacant lots, and backyards everywhere? I'm not talking about fairies and elves; I'm talking about insects and spiders. Most of these critters live their whole lives without being noticed. Once you start to look for them, though, you will be surprised at how easy they are to find. Just turn over a few leaves or walk through some tall weeds. Insects will crawl away or fly up before your eyes. These tiny crawlers and flyers of the animal kingdom are all around us, and it's a good thing. Without them, the world would not be habitable.

For example, if insects did not carry pollen from blossom to blossom, most flowering plants could not reproduce (see Bumblebee). And that's not all. Every kind of insect-eating animal (such as shrews, lizards, frogs, and fish) would soon starve, if the diet they depend on were to disappear.

Some insects are even important for what *they* eat. Certain species of beetles eat only rotting plants and dead animals (see Net-winged beetle). In so doing, they clean up the planet and prevent it from becoming a garbage dump.

Finally, there are insects that serve the earth by laying eggs in the soil (see Earwig). The young that hatch from these eggs remain underground for several years. There they eat and excrete nutrients, enriching the soil and readying it to receive seeds and grow healthy plants.

Without insects and spiders, life on earth would soon come to an end. Think of this the next time a mosquito buzzes around your head: You need the tiny beings that live in your yard.

See page 32 for more information.

A $\sim\sim\sim\sim\sim\sim\sim\sim\sim\sim\sim\sim\sim\sim\sim\sim\sim$ Ants and Aphids

In this picture some red ants are looking after tiny aphids. Ants take care of aphids, just as farmers take care of cows. When it rains, ants carry their aphids to shelter. When the weather clears, they bring them back outside to graze on plants. Red ants like the sweet-tasting juice that aphids make. To obtain some, all they need to do is tickle the aphids with their feelers.

Bumblebee ———————— B

This bumblebee has stuck its long tongue into a flower and is lapping up nectar. Bees and flowers need each other. When a bee feeds on a flower, its fuzzy body becomes coated with pollen. Some of this pollen will drop into the next blossom the bee visits. Flowers must exchange pollen in order to make seeds. Bees make this possible. In return, flowers provide bees with nectar.

C~~~~~~~~~~~~~~~~~~~~~~~~~ Crickets

Although crickets have wings, they don't fly. They don't need to. With their powerful hind legs, they can spring to safety in a series of long jumps. Crickets' wings have a use, though. When rubbed together they make a chirping sound. Most people like to hear this cheerful cricket talk. There are many kinds of crickets. The one shown here is a field cricket.

Dragonfly ～～～～～～～～～～～～～～～ D

A dragonfly is an amazing flyer. Its four wings work independently. This allows it to perform all kinds of midair maneuvers. While flying at top speed, it can suddenly reverse course and zoom backward. There are thousands of kinds of dragonflies in the world. All live near water and feed on newly hatched insects. This beautiful red dragonfly is called an Elisa skimmer.

E ∿∿∿∿∿∿∿∿∿∿∿∿∿∿∿∿∿∿∿∿∿∿∿∿∿∿∿∿∿∿∿∿∿∿∿ *Earwig*

During the day, earwigs hide under logs and stones. At night they come out and feed on tiny insects, plants, and ground litter. Female earwigs are attentive mothers. They lay their eggs in the soil and then guard them. They also bring food to their newly hatched babies, called nymphs. Earwigs do *not* crawl into people's ears, as some folks believe. Earwigs are quite harmless.

Fly ∿∿∿∿∿∿∿∿∿∿∿∿∿∿∿∿∿∿∿∿∿∿∿∿∿∿ F

The fly in this picture is using its strange-looking mouth to suck juice from a tomato. There are many kinds of flies. Most have big eyes that can see in many directions. Some flies bite animals or people and carry disease. Others destroy fruit crops. Not all flies are harmful, though. Some help farmers by eating other insects, and flies are an important food for birds and fish.

G ———————————————— Grasshopper

Grasshoppers come in several varieties. Some fly as well as leap. One kind gives off a bad smell to prevent predators from eating it. Another is called a locust. When locusts have eaten all the food in one area, they take off in a swarm to look for a new place to settle. Along the way, they drop down on farms and destroy entire crops. All grasshoppers have big appetites.

Hover fly ～～～～～～～～～～～～～～～～～～～～～～～ H

Here's a fly you can like. Did you think it was a wasp? Over long ages, the hover fly has come to resemble a stinging insect. This disguise warns predators to steer clear of it. Actually, the hover fly is harmless. It is even useful. During an early part of its life—a wormlike or larval stage—it gobbles up bugs that destroy plants. As an adult, it sips only flower nectar.

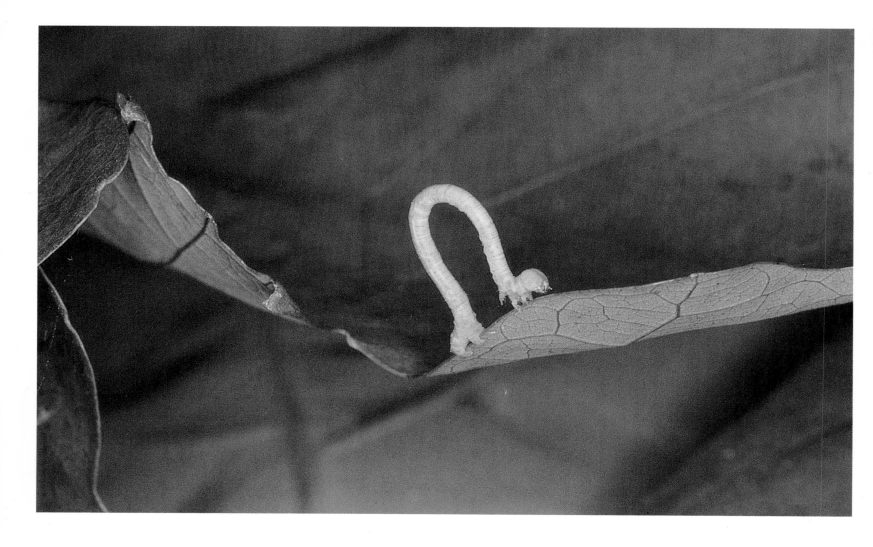

I ~~~~~~ Inchworm

This inchworm is going to be a moth someday. Right now it is a tiny caterpillar. It has an odd way of crawling. There are no legs along the middle part of its body, so it must loop along. To do this, the inchworm rears up on its back legs, stretches forward until it can grasp a leaf or a twig with its front legs, then brings its rear legs up to meet the front legs.

Japanese beetle ∼∼∼∼∼∼∼∼∼∼∼∼∼∼∼∼∼∼∼∼∼∼∼ J

This handsome beetle is not native to America. It came here from Japan in a shipment of iris bulbs. Now it has become so widespread that it is a pest. To get rid of this plant-eater, some gardeners release flies that feed on the Japanese beetle's larvae, which is better than spraying them with poison. Poison sprays are bad for people's health, and they also kill birds and useful insects.

K ～～～～～～～～～～～～～～～～～～～ Katydid

The katydid is named for its mating call: "katy DID, katy DID." Occasionally, one sings out: "katy DIDN'T!" On chilly nights katydids chant slowly. As the temperature rises, they step up the pace. Only males take part in the chorus. They're trying to attract females to tree branches where the males sit hidden. Katydids are hard to see. Their green bodies look just like leaves.

$\mathcal{L}$acewing ∼∼∼∼∼∼∼∼∼∼∼∼∼∼∼∼∼∼∼∼∼∼∼∼∼∼∼∼∼∼∼∼ L

The lacewing is a tiny insect with long, see-through wings. It is found on blades of grass and weeds. Lacewings lay eggs that hatch into larvae, called aphid lions. Farmers and gardeners are glad to have aphid lions around because they eat bugs that destroy crops and flowers. In time, aphid lions wrap themselves in silk cocoons and slowly change into beautiful adult lacewings.

M~~~~~~~Mosquito

Only the female mosquito bites. She needs a meal of blood to produce eggs. She lays her eggs in water, where they hatch into wrigglers. Wrigglers must live in water while they grow wings. One way to control mosquito numbers is to drain flowerpots and sprinkling cans so that female mosquitoes find fewer places in which to lay eggs. Some kinds of mosquitoes carry diseases.

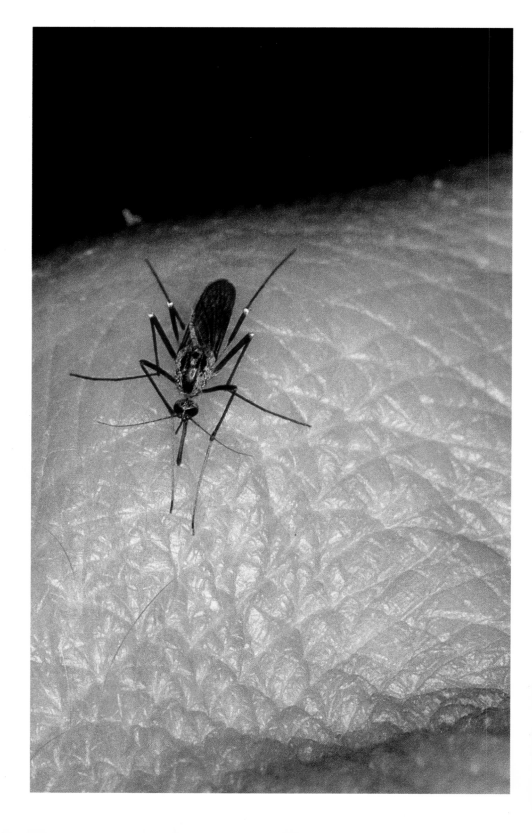

Net-winged beetle ~~~~~~~~~~~~~~~~~~~~~~~~~~~~~~~~~~~~ N

There are 300,000 different kinds of beetles in the world. Some are tiny, some are big. Some are beautiful, some are dull. This net-winged beetle has bright orange markings that warn birds not to eat it. A meal of netwings would make a bird sick. Certain moths wear the netwing's colors and fool hungry birds. You can find this insect on dying flowers. It feeds on rotting plants.

O~~~~~~~~~~~~~~~~~~~~~~~~~Orange sulphur butterfly

When at rest the orange sulphur, like most butterflies, holds its wings upright
and together. That is one way to tell a butterfly from a moth. When a moth
rests, it curls its wings around its body or folds them neatly across its back.
Orange sulphurs spend their days flitting about sunny meadows. By contrast,
most moths come out after dark.

Praying mantis ～～～P

A praying mantis hunts other insects and is itself hard to find. It hides on plants and looks like a green leaf. When an insect lands in reach of its powerful front legs, a mantis pounces. Then it eats its victim head first. This insect has a huge appetite. It can finish off a big grasshopper or a dragonfly in a single meal. A female praying mantis will even eat her mate.

Q ~~~~~~~~~~~~~~~~~~~~~~~~~~~~~~~~~~~~~ Queen butterfly

This colorful butterfly lives in parts of the United States where the weather is mild. When in flight, it keeps its long tongue, called a proboscis, tightly coiled. To sip nectar, it unfurls this long drinking straw and inserts it into a blossom. Queen is this butterfly's common name: Males as well as females are called queens.

Robber fly ———————————————— R

The robber fly hunts and kills other insects. It pounces on crawlers and flyers of all kinds and quickly devours them. Even the larvae of this predator fly feed on insects found in the soil. Some kinds of robber flies are specialists and hunt only bees. Others eat almost anything: flying ants, bugs, grasshoppers, moths—and other flies.

S~~~~~~Spider

Did you know that spiders are not insects? They have eight legs—two more than true insects have. Not all of the 35,000 species of spiders in the world create webs for trapping food. Some use the silk they spin to make egg sacs, which they attach to twigs. Spiders make bungee jumps off high places. While dropping, they spin out a line of strong silk from which to dangle.

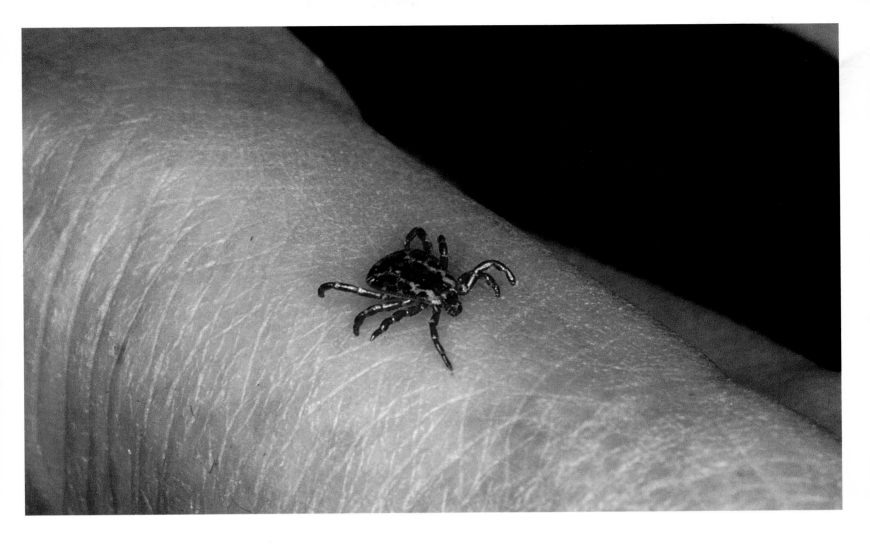

Tick ～～～～～～～～～～～～～～～～～～～～～ T

Like their spider relatives, ticks have eight legs and are not insects. Ticks feed on the blood of mammals, reptiles, and birds. A tick will wait on a blade of grass until a likely meal brushes against it. Then it attaches itself to the passerby. Some tick species carry diseases. That's why you should always remove a tick from your skin as soon as you discover it.

U———————Underwing moth

The hind wings of the underwing moth are beautifully colored. By contrast, its front wings are dull and look like tree bark. When at rest on a tree, this moth covers its gorgeous hind wings with its barklike front wings and so blends with its background. In this way, it makes itself invisible to birds that would eat it. You may have walked past an underwing moth without noticing it.

Violet tail ━━━━━━〜〜〜〜〜〜〜〜〜〜〜〜〜〜〜〜〜〜〜〜〜〜〜〜〜〜〜〜〜━━ V

The violet tail is a tiny, delicate damselfly, hardly more than an inch long. Damselflies are often mistaken for dragonflies, but they are different. Damselfly eyes are on stalks, like flowers; dragonflies have eyes that are set in their heads. All species of damselfly rest with their wings held back. Dragonfly species hold their wings outstretched, like airplanes.

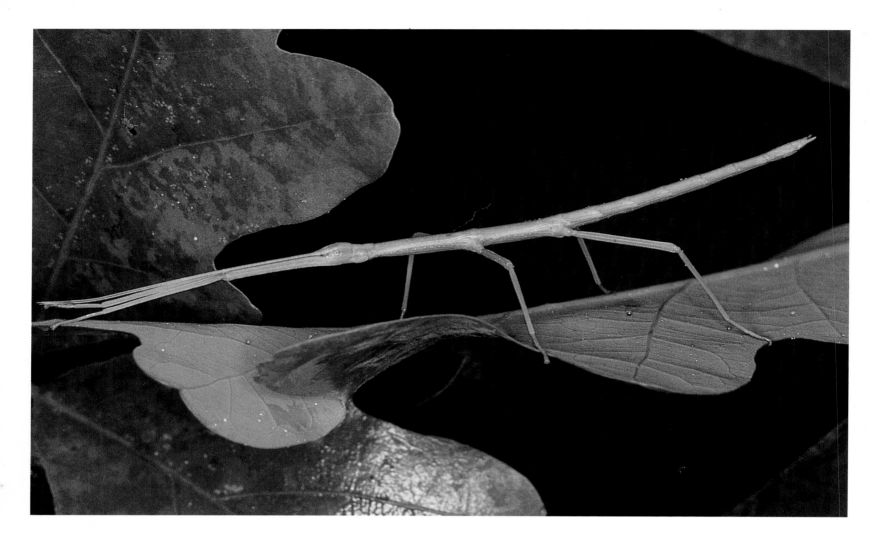

W ∼∼∼∼∼∼∼∼∼∼∼∼∼∼∼∼∼∼∼∼∼∼∼∼ Walking stick

Did you ever see a stick get up and move? If so, you have met this strange creature. A walking stick is beautifully camouflaged to protect it from hungry birds. During the day it remains as still as a twig so as not to be noticed. At night it feeds on leaves. When a walking stick loses a leg, it is able to grow a new one. Newly hatched walking sticks are green.

X-back (little milkweed bug) ∼∼∼∼∼∼∼∼∼∼∼∼∼∼∼∼ X

You'll know the little milkweed bug by the X on its back. It eats poisonous milkweed seeds. As a result of this diet, it too is poisonous. Any bird that eats the little milkweed bug will sicken or die. Most birds seem to know this. They are alerted by the red X on its back—a kind of skull-and-crossbones warning label. Red is used by many insects to signal danger.

Y ∼∼∼∼∼∼∼∼∼∼∼∼∼∼∼∼∼∼∼∼∼∼∼∼∼∼∼∼∼∼∼ Yellowjacket

The yellowjacket is a social wasp. A colony of yellowjackets consists almost entirely of females. One queen lays all the eggs, and her adult daughters tend all the offspring. In late summer a few males hatch from special eggs. After mating, they die, as do unmated females. Only mated females winter over to start new underground colonies the next spring. This wasp's sting is painful.

Zebra longwing butterfly —————————————— Z

This butterfly is striped like a zebra. It isn't as swift as a zebra, though. It wafts through the air like a feather. The zebra longwing is able to make a tiny creaking noise by wriggling its body. It likes a warm climate and thrives in the Florida Everglades. At night large numbers of zebra longwings gather and roost together in trees.

Some Hints on How to Find the Critters in This Book

(All photographs are enlarged. Actual sizes are given below.)

Ant - 3/8 inch - This kind of ant lives near poplar trees. The aphids it keeps must drink poplar sap.

Bumblebee - 1/2 inch - Bees are easy to find when trees blossom and flowers are in bloom.

Cricket - 1 inch - Some crickets enter houses. This kind lives outside under boards and stones.

Dragonfly - 1 1/4 inch - Look for dragonflies flying over ponds and streams or resting on shore plants.

Earwig - 3/4 inch - This insect hides in dark spaces during the day. I found one in my garage.

Fly - 1/4 inch - Flies can be anywhere, indoors or out. Horses use their tails to switch them away.

Grasshopper - 1 1/4 inch - Watch for them in dry fields and roadsides. They make a buzz when they leap.

Hover fly - 3/8 inch - Look for this pretty insect on wildflowers. It could be mistaken for a tiny bee.

Inchworm - 1 inch - This little caterpillar might spend some time in your vegetable garden.

Japanese beetle - 1/2 inch - Here's a beetle that likes to eat leaves. Its shiny back will catch your eye.

Katydid - 2 inches - You may not see this noisy fellow. It lives high in trees. But you will hear it.

Lacewing - 1/2 inch - If you have good eyes, you will spot this tiny insect on plants and bushes.

Mosquito - 1/4 inch - You won't have to go looking for a mosquito. It will find you!

Netwing - 3/8 inch - Netwings feed on dead plants and rotten fruit that has fallen from trees.

Orange sulphur - 2 inches - This butterfly flits from flower to flower. Look for it in a field.

Praying mantis - 2 1/2 inches - A good hider, the praying mantis is easy to miss. It looks like a plant.

Queen - 3 1/4 inches - Don't hunt for this milkweed-eater unless you live in the South. It likes warmth.

Robber fly - 1 inch - Where many insects gather to feed on plants, this predator is sure to drop in.

Spider - 1/2 inch - To find a spider, look for a fresh web, touch it, and a spider will appear.

Tick - 1/8 inch - You might not see a tick until you feel it crawling on you.

Underwing - 3 inches - To find this moth, which looks like tree bark, inspect tree trunks.

Violet tail - 1 1/8 inch - All damselflies live near water, but only one is violet colored.

Walking stick - 3 1/2 inches - When a stick moves, study it closely—especially after a rainstorm.

X-back (little milkweed bug) - 1/2 inch - Look for this bug on milkweed. That's the only thing it eats.

Yellowjacket - 1/2 inch - Listen for a buzzing sound and keep your distance. Yellowjackets sting!

Zebra longwing - 3 1/4 inches - This butterfly dislikes cold winters. Only Southerners will find it.

Note:
The insect on the title page is a ladybug - 1/4 inch.
The bug on the back cover is a scarlet and green leafhopper - 3/8 inch.